# Railways & Recollections
## 1962

**SANDHURST HALT:** Like most folk in southern England, residents of the Berkshire town of Sandhurst awoke on 2 January to a blizzard. This was the scene at Sandhurst Halt as the 11.05 from Reading arrives, hauled by 'N' Class No 31872.

# Contents

## Acknowledgements

We would like to record our gratitude to the late Ray Ruffell – railwayman and cameraman extraordinaire. Realising that his beloved steam engines were about to disappear from Britain's railways for ever, he made it his personal mission to get out to record them at every opportunity. Both at work on the Southern Region and on excursions to all corners of the country, he clicked away, taking some of the most atmospheric railways shots of the era.

Without his photographs, this book would not have been possible.

Thank you, Ray.

First published in 2011

# Introduction:
## Times of chills and change...

1962 began and ended in Arctic conditions. It opened with Britain enveloped in heavy snow and ended with the coldest winter in living memory. Yet unlike today, when it seems a few flakes of snow send the entire transport network into turmoil, the trains kept going – just like they always did in the good old days.

Yet 1962 was a year of massive change for both Britain and its railways. On the latter, it was the last year in which British Railways steam locomotives outnumbered their diesel and electric counterparts. They already had in the Eastern Region, which by 1962 had just 32 steam depots remaining. In 1959 it had been 69. Among those that had been demolished the previous year was my local shed, King's Lynn (31C), which was demolished using the pulling power of the last of the 'J17' 0-6-0 tender locos that had so long been associated with the place. I expect the top brass used the faithful steam loco because they couldn't yet trust the unreliable Brush Type 2 diesel locomotives that had been sent to replace them (one of the latter actually broke down while hauling the Royal Train).

In fact, 1962 was the year that saw the biggest upheaval to the nation's transport system since nationalisation in 1947. The Transport Act of 1962 saw the break-up of the British Transport Commission into five new public authorities – British Railways Board, British Transport Docks Board, British Waterways Board, London Transport Board and Transport Holding Company.

But worse was to come, because the effects of Dr Beeching's report – *The Re-Shaping of British Railways* – would strike at the heart of the system in the following years. A third of the network would be axed in five years, together with more than 2,000 stations and 67,000 jobs

Printed and bound in Česká Republika

British Library Cataloguing in Publication Data
A catalogue record for this book is available from the British Library.

ISBN 978 1 85794 375 7
Silver Link Publishing Ltd
The Trundle
Ringstead Road
Great Addington
Kettering
Northants NN14 4BW

Tel/Fax: 01536 330588
email: sales@nostalgiacollection.com
Website: www.nostalgiacollection.com

in British Railways. Wouldn't modern, congested Britain be a very different place if we still had that wonderful system of public transport? But back in 1962 we had other issues on our minds…

A high pressure system in early December saw a blanket of fog descend on the country, which in the built-up cities and industrial towns meant smog – the deadly combination of fog and fumes from burning fossil fuels. By 6 December 90 people had already died, while London's Emergency Bed Service said that 235 people had been admitted to hospital in the previous 24 hours and issued a red warning to prepare for more admissions. The Ministry of Health warned people with chest and heart complaints to stay indoors and advised others to wear masks or wrap a scarf around their mouths and noses.

For drivers, visibility was often down to zero. It was the worst since the so-called 'Great Smog' of 1952, in which 4,000 lives were lost – and which had led to the Clean Air Act of 1952.

But the biggest threat to human life came in the autumn of 1962, with the Cuban Missiles Crisis. It began in September, when Russia secretly agreed to send nuclear missiles to the Caribbean island of Cuba, following the Bay of Pigs incident – an unsuccessful operation by the USA to overthrow Cuba's communist regime.

On 14 October a US U-2 spy plane high above Cuba took pictures of Soviet missiles being installed, leading to the world's greatest superpowers going head-to-head in a confrontation that could so easily have led to the horror of a nuclear war.

The Cuban missiles were within range of most of America's major cities, which the Soviets considered reasonable since America had already installed nuclear missiles in Turkey, capable of striking Moscow. It was a deadly stalemate.

On 22 October, in a televised address, US President John F. Kennedy announced to the nation the existence of Soviet missiles in Cuba. Privately, he weighed up his options and even considered a full-scale military attack, but eventually settled upon a military blockade of the island and demanded that the Soviets removed the weapons.

Two days later came the first confrontation between the US Navy and a Soviet cargo vessel. The world held its breath, but the vessel changed course. Meanwhile, behind the scenes, Kennedy and his Soviet counterpart, Nikita Khrushchev, brokered a deal in which the USSR would remove its missiles from Cuba if the US did the same in Turkey. The Soviets begin dismantling their missiles in Cuba on 1 November and the US blockade ended on the 20th. The crisis was over.

On a lighter note, 1962 was the year that the Beatles auditioned for Decca – and were rejected. The record company learned from its mistakes, however, and signed up the Rolling Stones a few months later. The Swinging Sixties were about to start swinging, but the old order reigned in the charts, with Cliff Richard's *The Young Ones* at No 1 as the year opened, and Elvis Presley seeing out 1962 with *Return To*

*Sender*, his fourth chart-topper of the year.

In the world of sport, newly promoted Ipswich Town won the First Division championship at their first attempt, led by their promising young manager, Alf Ramsey, who would of course lead England to even greater things in 1966. Meanwhile, Tottenham Hotspur won the FA Cup and Norwich City lifted the League Cup.

While the railways were decimated by the short-term thinking of an unimaginative government and its public servants, the latter indulged in a frenzied spree of road building, with 1962 seeing the M5 motorway completed between Birmingham and Gloucestershire, and the M6 extended to Stafford.

But all those roads would prove pretty useless as the year drew to a close. That zero-visibility smog of early December was followed by the coldest winter in living memory. On 22 December the temperature dropped below zero and there wasn't a single frost-free night between then and 5 March the following year. Britain was gripped by Arctic-like conditions and roads were either blocked by snowdrifts or treacherous as skating rinks. But the trains, as always, kept going, as this book demonstrates…

David Phillips
Northamptonshire
May 2011

# JANUARY and there's a chill in the air...

**SANDHURST HALT:** The same station as seen in our opening picture and the same day, but another train – this time an express from Redhill, headed by 'N' Class 2-6-0 No 31851. Some 80 of these engines were built at the South Eastern & Chatham Railway's Ashford Works between 1917 and 1934. The SECR was amalgamated into the Southern Railway at the Grouping of 1923.

**SANDHURST HALT:** The conditions are no better the following day, as another 'N' Class 2-6-0 (number unknown) stops at a red signal. Fireman Johnny Reynolds of Reading depot is obeying Rule 55, which stated that if a train was brought to a stand at a signal, within 3 minutes in clear weather or immediately in rain, snow or fog, the driver of the train must dispatch his fireman (or guard) to the signal box to ensure that the signalman was aware of the presence of the train, and that all safeguards to protect the train, such as slides or collars on the signal levers, were in place; the crewman would then sign the train register to confirm this. Despite the Arctic-like conditions, the fireman would no doubt have welcomed the respite from his hard graft on the footplate, provided the signal box wasn't too far away…

**REDHILL:** There's still snow in evidence between the tracks on Sunday 14 January as yet another 'N' Class 2-6-0, this time No 31863, heads out of Redhill hauling a special on a crisp winter's morning.

**CARDIGAN:** Over in West Wales 0-6-0 pannier tank No 1613 is shunting the yard at Cardigan, while 2-6-2 tank engine No 4558 waits to depart with a two-coach local service.

**WOKINGHAM:** The 11.33am freight from Reading storms through Wokingham en route to Feltham, hauled by an unidentified member of arguably the greatest 0-6-0 tender engine class ever built – the 'Q1'. Some 40 of these so-called 'austerity' engines were built during the Second World War, to the design of the Southern Railway's Chief Mechanical Engineer, Oliver Bulleid. Weighing 90 tons, each loco had a tractive effort of more than 30,000lb, which it put down on the rails through six coupled wheels of 5ft 1in diameter.

# 1962 Happenings (1)

**January**
- BBC screens first episode of the long-running police drama *Z Cars*
- 93 die in Holland's worst rail disaster, at Harmelen
- Ranger 3 is launched to study the Moon, but misses by 22,000 miles

**February**
- The *Sunday Times* becomes the first paper to print a colour supplement
- American pilot Francis Gary Powers is exchanged for captured Soviet spy Rudolf Abel
- Ballet stars Margot Fonteyn and Rudolf Nureyev dance together in London

**March**
- France and Algeria sign an agreement in Évian-les-Bains ending the Algerian War
- *Un Premier Amour*, sung by Isabelle Aubret, wins the Eurovision Song Contest

**April**
- Jawaharlal Nehru is elected Prime Minister of India
- James Hanratty is hanged in Bedford Gaol for the A6 murder
- *West Side Story* wins Best Picture at the 34th Academy Awards
- The Commonwealth Immigration Bill removes free immigration for the citizens of member states of the Commonwealth
- Ranger 4 spacecraft crashes into the Moon

# FEBRUARY calling at Uxbridge, Waterloo Exeter and the North East...

*Right* **UXBRIDGE:** Venerable visitors in Uxbridge yard on 1 February are Great Western '1400' Class 0-4-2T engine No 1474 and a GW brake-van. Like the other 74 members of this class, No 1474 was built at Swindon Works, between 1932 and 1936. They were designed for branch-line passenger work, but were pressed into freight and shunting duties too. They were all withdrawn by 1965 and four were preserved (but not this engine).

*Below* **UXBRIDGE:** A three-car diesel multiple unit is about to leave, forming the 9.11am service to Paddington. Early DMUs like this Derby Lightweight were painted with 'speed whiskers' on the front panel, which were already being replaced by solid yellow warning panels.

**WATERLOO:** Driver Moody of Eastleigh depot waits for the signal to depart for the West Country with 'Merchant Navy' Class 4-6-2 No 35017 *Belgian Marine*. This loco entered service in April 1945, was rebuilt in March 1957 and was scrapped in July 1966.

**EXETER:** On Sunday 18 February 'West Country' Class 4-6-2 'light Pacific'
No 34033 *Chard* is about to depart for the West with the second portion of an
express that has recently arrived from Waterloo. Built at Brighton in July 1946,
No 34033 was scrapped in December 1965.

*Below* **NEWCASTLE:** Our photographer headed north to Tyneside on 22 February, where he captured ex-LNER 'Q6' Class 0-8-0 No 63381 heading through Newcastle with a train of loaded hoppers. This class of 120 heavy freight locomotives was designed by Vincent Raven and built at Darlington Works between 1913 and 1921. Most were withdrawn between 1963 and 1967, and only one was preserved.

*Right:* **NEWCASTLE:** Seen from the same vantage point, this time 'J27' 0-6-0 No 65861 is hauling an up freight. Designed for the North Eastern Railway by Wilson Worsdell, 115 of these engines were built between 1906 and 1922, although many modifications were carried out in subsequent years. One has survived into preservation.

*Below:* **NEWCASTLE:** On pilot duties this day is 'V3' 2-6-2T No 67651. Sir Nigel Gresley designed this engine and the very similar 'V1' for the LNER. A total of 82 'V1s' were built between 1930 and 1939, with ten 'V3s' added between 1939 and 1940. The main difference between the two was that the 'V3' had a higher boiler pressure and was thus more powerful.

**WIMBLEDON:** It's a case of Southern Electric at Wimbledon Park depot on 23 February, when our photographer scrambled to the top of a bank to capture this photo of the massed ranks of EMUs. He estimates that there were 80 cars in all.

# MARCH Western pilgrimage, Southern seaside and sheds...

**CHARD:** It's 9 March and we're in Somerset now, where ex-Great Western '5700' Class 0-6-0PT No 3669 is forming the 1.35pm local stopping service from Chard Central to Taunton. This little pannier tank loco was once one of the most familiar sights on Britain's railways, for a staggering 863 were built between 1929 and 1950 (by far the majority at GWR's Swindon Works), designed by Charles Collett. A total of 16 have survived into preservation, including two at the Didcot Railway Centre.

**TAUNTON:**
'Castle' Class No 5014 *Goodrich Castle* returns to the loco depot. The GWR's 'Castle' Class locos were designed by the company's Chief Mechanical Engineer, Charles Collett; 171 were built at Swindon between 1923 and 1950, and became legendary for their performance. On 6 June 1932 one of the class – No 5006 *Tregenna Castle* – set an average speed of 81.68mph between Swindon and Paddington, which was a world record at the time. Eight have survived into preservation, including two at Didcot Railway Centre (a must-visit place for Great Western fans).

**SWINDON:** This picture, taken on 18 March, may not mean much to the uninitiated, but railway enthusiasts will realise why photographer Ray leaned out of the window of the passing Weston-super-Mare express to snap this scene at Swindon – probably the greatest railway workshop in the world. Standing outside is a BR Standard 5 4-6-0 awaiting overhaul, while a forlorn-looking 'King' Class loco faces a very doubtful future.

**WATERLOO:** It seems also like sacrilege to see electric motive power standing at the hallowed platforms of London's Waterloo station – the spiritual home of the greatest steam locomotives ever built by the Southern Railway. But motorman Piercey of Farnham, a former driver of steam locos, looks happy enough. He's about to set off with a service heading for Alton and Portsmouth.

*Right* **GUILDFORD:** Here's something a bit different – ex-LSWR 'M7' Class 0-4-4T No 30132, standing at Guildford. The stovepipe chimney marks this out as a remnant of a past era – and it is. Designed by Dugald Drummond, 105 of these engines were built between 1897 and 1911 at Nine Elms (95) and Eastleigh (10) to answer the call for more power and speed on suburban passenger services.

*Left* **GUILDFORD:** Snapped at Guildford loco depot on 26 March is the venerable shed pilot, ex-LSWR 'B4' dock tank No 30089. Twenty-five of these engines were built between 1891 and 1908, to a design by William Adams. Two have survived into preservation, including one on the Bluebell Railway in Sussex.

*Left* **GUILDFORD:** Another ex-LSWR 0-4-4T, this time 'M7' No 30378, heads a local service to Horsham. This locomotive is fitted with a Westinghouse brake.

*Left, main picture* **BOURNEMOUTH:** One of Southern's crack expresses, the 'Bournemouth Belle', arrives at Bournemouth Central from Waterloo with its plush Pullman coaches pulled by 'Merchant Navy' Class 'Pacific' No 35029 *Ellerman Lines*. Built in 1949, this engine was rebuilt in 1959 and eventually retired in September 1966. You can still see it today – as an exhibit at the National Railway Museum, York. Meanwhile, 'West Country' Class 'light Pacific' No 34006 *Bude* waits with an express back to the capital. Sadly, this locomotive was not preserved.

*Below* **GUILDFORD:** In this atmospheric view of the roundhouse at Guildford loco, 'N' Class No 31864 is being turned on the turntable. A total of 131 of these locomotives were built between 1917 and 1934.

## 1962 Happenings (2)

**May**
- Norwich City wins the English League Cup, beating Rochdale in the final
- 160 die in a triple-train disaster near Tokyo
- 12 East Germans escape via a tunnel under the Berlin Wall
- Juan Carlos of Spain marries the Greek Princess Sophia in Athens
- The new Coventry Cathedral is consecrated

**June**
- Acker Bilk's *Stranger On The Shore* becomes the first British record to reach No 1 in the US charts
- Frank Morris, John Anglin and Clarence Anglin escape from the Alcatraz Island prison
- BBC's *Steptoe and Son* makes its debut
- Brazil beats Czechoslovakia 3-1 to win the 1962 World Cup
- An Air France Boeing 707 jet crashes in Guadeloupe, killing all 113 on board. It is the airline's second fatal accident in just three weeks, and the third fatal 707 crash of the year

**July**
- American artist Andy Warhol premieres his Campbell's Soup Cans exhibit in Los Angeles
- Telstar, the world's first commercial communications satellite, is launched into orbit and later in the month relays the first trans-Atlantic television signal
- The Rolling Stones make their debut at London's Marquee Club
- Prime Minister Harold Macmillan dismisses a third of his Cabinet

Left **CHESSINGTON:** Driver Vic McCaughie poses at Chessington South before taking electric multiple unit No 4110 to Waterloo.

Below **GUILDFORD:** Maunsell 'S15' 4-6-0 No 30824 simmers gently at Guildford. Designed by Robert Urie, 45 of these engines were built at Eastleigh Works between 1920 and 1936. Seven of the class have been preserved, including three on Hampshire's Watercress Line.

# APRIL Oiling the wheels of industry...

*Below* **GUILDFORD:** Driver 'Jas' Taylor and guard Crane are happy to pose for a photograph before leaving for Reading with a train headed by 'U' Class No 31630. This class of 50 2-6-0 engines was designed by Richard Maunsell for passenger work and was heavily influenced by the contemporary locomotives of the Great Western Railway, designed by George Churchward. The 'U' Class engines were built between 1928 and 1931 at Ashford, Brighton and Eastleigh.

*Right* **GUILDFORD:** Another photo of driver Taylor and No 31630, topping up the motion gear ports with oil before leaving for Reading.

Below **PORTSMOUTH:** Ray captioned this photograph 'Dignity and Impudence'. We presume the dignity belongs to BR 4MT 4-6-0 No 75078, while 'A1' 32678, seen again, is the impudent one! Both seem happy enough in adjacent berths at Fratton loco. Fifty 'Terriers' were built between 1872 and 1880 at Brighton Works for the London, Brighton & South Coast Railway, to the design of William Stroudley. By coincidence, No 75078 was built at Brighton, too.

Above **PORTSMOUTH:** Class 'A1' 0-6-0T tank engine No 32678 is at Fratton loco on 20 April. This engine, like others in its class, nicknamed 'Terriers', was built in 1880 and withdrawn in October 1963. Originally sold to Butlin's, where it was used as a static display at the company's holiday camp in Minehead, Somerset, it was later sold to the West Somerset Railway in 1975, which in turn sold it to Resco (Railways) Ltd in 1983. It lives on in preservation.

# 1960 ARRIVALS AND DEPARTURES

## ARRIVALS

| Name | Occupation | Date |
|---|---|---|
| Jim Carrey | Actor and comedian | 17 January |
| Sam Phillips | Singer | 28 January |
| Axl Rose | Rock musician | 6 February |
| Garth Brooks | Country singer | 7 February |
| Sheryl Crow | Singer | 11 February |
| Lou Diamond Phillips | Actor | 17 February |
| Vanessa Feltz | TV presenter | 21 February |
| Jon Bon Jovi | Rock musician | 2 March |
| Sir Steve Redgrave | Rower | 23 March |
| MC Hammer | Rap singer | 30 March |
| Philip Schofield | TV presenter | 1 April |
| Vincent Gallo | Actor | 11 April |
| Jimmy White | Snooker player | 2 May |
| Danny Huston | Film director | 14 May |
| Paula Abdul | Singer and dancer | 19 June |
| Amanda Donohoe | Actress | 29 June |
| Tom Cruise | Actor | 3 July |
| Neil Morrissey | Actor | 4 July |
| Pam Shriver | Tennis player | 4 July |
| Wesley Snipes | Actor | 31 July |
| Ruud Gullit | Footballer | 1 September |
| Jack Dee | Comedian | 24 September |
| Ally McCoist | Footballer | 24 September |
| Evander Holyfield | Boxer | 19 October |
| Nick Hancock | Actor and TV presenter | 25 October |
| Sharron Davies | Swimmer | 1 November |
| Demi Moore | Actress | 11 November |
| Jodie Foster | Actress | 19 November |
| Ralph Fiennes | Actor | 22 December |

## DEPARTURES

|  |  |  |
|---|---|---|
| 'Lucky' Luciano | American gangster (b1897) | 26 January |
| Eduard von Steiger | President of Switzerland (b1881) | 10 February |
| Halliwell Hobbes | English actor (b1877) | 20 February |
| Arthur Compton | Physicist (b1892) | 15 March |
| Stuart Sutcliffe | Ex-Beatle (b1940) | 10 April |
| Sir Frederick Handley Page | Aircraft manufacturer (b1885) | 21 April |
| Vita Sackville-West | Landscape gardener (b1892) | 2 June |
| William Faulkner | Writer (b1897) | 6 July |
| Marilyn Monroe | Actress (b1926) | 5 August |
| Graham Walker | Motorcycle racer (b1896) | 7 September |
| Eleanor Roosevelt | US First Lady (b1884) | 7 November |
| Queen Wilhelmina | Netherlands (b1880) | 28 November |
| Charles Laughton | Actor and director (b1899) | 15 December |

# MAY/JUNE

## The summer now approaching...

**GUILDFORD:** It's 9 May and this photograph depicts 'N' Class 2-6-0 No 31842 descending Guildford Bank with the 9.11am freight from Reading.

**GUILDFORD:** Same day, same place, only this time it's 'N' Class 2-6-0 No 31862 climbing the bank at just 10mph after a dead stand at Guildford with the 600-ton ex-Redhill freight.

**GUILDFORD:** A day later and another assault on the bank, this time with 'N' Class 31858 hauling the heavy ex-Redhill freight. The driver is J. Hewitt.

*Below* **GUILDFORD:** Ex-LMS Class 2 2-6-2T No 41303 leaves Guildford with a passenger service to Horsham on the evening of 15 May.

*Right* **DORKING:** Drivers of heaving freight trains tackling the steep Dorking Bank were happy to be in charge of a 'Q1', the most powerful 0-6-0 ever built. No 33033, with Reading driver Girdler, is storming up the final part of the bank, near Welcome Bridge, on 17 May.

# JULY calling at Dorking, Southampton...

## 1962 No 1 Records

**January**
Cliff Richard & The Shadows *The Young Ones*

**February**
Elvis Presley *Rock-A-Hula-Baby / Can't Help Falling In Love*

**March**
The Shadows *Wonderful Land*

**May**
B. Bumble & The Stingers *Nut Rocker*
Elvis Presley *Good Luck Charm*

**June**
Mike Sarne (featuring Wendy Richard) *Come Outside*

**July**
Ray Charles *I Can't Stop Loving You*
Frank Ifield *I Remember You*

**September**
Elvis Presley *She's Not You*

**October**
Tornados *Telstar*

**November**
Frank Ifield *Lovesick Blues*

**December**
Elvis Presley *Return To Sender*

*Right* **DORKING:** 'M' Class 2-6-0 No 31414 passes Welcome Bridge near the summit of Dorking Bank, between Dorking and Comshall.

*Below* **SOUTHAMPTON:** Ex-LBSCR 'E2' Class 0-6-0T No 32109 shunts empty stock in Southampton New Docks on 1 July.

**LYME REGIS:** Driver Woodman of Lyme Regis and his young fireman pose beside 2-6-2T No 41299 at Lyme Regis before heading off for Axminster on a stopping local passenger service.

*Top right* **HORSHAM:** Ex-LMS Class 2 2-6-2T No 41260 takes a drink at Horsham loco depot on 6 July.

*Right* **SANDHURST:** Ex-Great Western 'Manor' Class 4-6-0 No 7808 *Cookham Manor* is about to leave Sandhurst for Reading with a passenger service from Redhill.

*Right* **SOUTHAMPTON:** 'Merchant Navy' Class 4-6-2 No 35027 *Port Line* stands at Southampton Central, about to depart with the 4.15pm service to Waterloo.

*Below* **HORSHAM:** 'Q' Class 0-6-0 No 30546 receives attention at Horsham loco depot.

*Below right* **CLAPHAM JUNCTION:** It's probably the most famous railway junction in the world – and BR Standard Class 4 2-6-4T No 80064 is leaving it on the Oxted line. The photographer took this great picture while leaning precariously from a swaying van on a Waterloo to Chessington train!

**SALISBURY:** 'Merchant Navy' Class 4-6-2 No 35010 *Blue Star* departs from the Wiltshire cathedral city with the up 'Atlantic Coast Express' on 14 July. Built at the height of the Second World War, in 1942, this engine performed for BR until September 1966. Today it is in storage at the Colne Valley Railway, awaiting restoration.

**WOLVERTON:** We're on ex-LMS tracks now on the West Coast Main Line in Buckinghamshire. It's hard to believe the nonchalance of the young lads on the platform as No 71000 *Duke of Gloucester* coasts into Wolverton with a stopping train. Are they so used to legendary locomotives that they don't realise that this is the one and only BR Standard Class 8 locomotive ever constructed? Build at Crewe Works in 1954 to the design of Robert Riddles, the engine was a replacement for the 'Princess Royal' Class loco *Princess Anne*, which had been destroyed in the Harrow & Wealdstone rail disaster in 1952.

Unfortunately, *Duke of Gloucester* was a poor performer with heavy fuel consumption and no further examples of the class were built. It was withdrawn after eight years, but a group of enthusiasts rescued it from Barry scrapyard in South Wales and spent 13 years restoring it. At the same time they carried out modifications that turned it into one of the most powerful steam locomotives in Britain. Watching it today on one of its main-line excursions, you can be excused for thinking 'if only…'

# AUGUST Coast to coast, west to south…

Below **WOLVERTON:** We're still on the West Coast Main Line as this northbound passenger train – comprising at least 16 coaches – passes through. It's headed by 'Coronation' Class No 46252 *City of Leicester;* designed by William Stanier, 38 of these powerful express 'Pacifics' were built at the LMS Crewe Works between 1937 and 1948.

*Left* **BLETCHLEY:** A few miles up the line at Bletchley, 'Jinty' 0-6-0T No 47500 is on station pilot duties. Back in 1962 there would have been pleasant green fields between the small towns of Wolverton and Bletchley... today there is the urban sprawl of Milton Keynes. 'Jinty' was the nickname for these ex-LMS Fowler Class 3Fs, of which 422 were built between 1924 and 1931.

# 1962 Happenings (3)

**August**
- Marilyn Monroe dies from an overdose of sleeping pills
- Nelson Mandela is arrested and charged with incitement to rebellion
- Beatles drummer Pete Best is fired and replaced by Ringo Starr
- A failed assassination attempt is made against French President Charles De Gaulle
- John Lennon secretly marries Cynthia Powell

**September**
- The first Cortina rolls off Ford's production line at Dagenham
- The Soviet Union agrees to send arms to Cuba
- Glasgow Corporation runs its last trams
- A flash flood in Barcelona kills more than 440 people

**October**
- *Dr No*, the first James Bond film, premieres in UK theatres
- The Beatles release their first single for EMI, *Love Me Do*
- Pictures of Soviet missile silos in Cuba, taken by US spy planes, spark the Cuba Missiles Crisis and a stand-off between the USA and the USSR that leaves the superpowers on the brink of nuclear war
  The Fab Four make their TV debut on *People and Places*

**BLETCHLEY:** While at Bletchley, photographer Ray couldn't resist a peek into the loco depot, where he found ex-LNWR 0-8-0s Nos 49093, 49106 and 49287 in storage. Looking out of place alongside is a Metro-Cammell DMU.

**BUCKINGHAM:** Single-unit railcar No 79906 is waiting for passengers at Buckingham. Meanwhile, a Class 4 4-6-0 on local freight duties hovers in the background.

**OXFORD:** Ex-GWR No 7011 *Banbury Castle* arrives at Oxford at the head of the 'Cathedrals Express'.

**GUILDFORD:** The loco yard at Guildford was so close to the station that it was possible for bystanders to get a good view of what was going on. Our photographer stood at the end of Platform 8 to capture this scene on Sunday 12 August, with 'Q1' No 33005 getting its smokebox cleaned. Other engines in sight include 'N' Class 2-6-0 No 31811, 'Q1' No 33032, 'U' 2-6-0 No 31800, and a couple more unidentified 'Q1s' waiting for coal.

*Above* **BOURNEMOUTH:** 'Merchant Navy' Class No 35020 *Bibby Line* receives attention at Bournemouth loco depot on 18 August prior to working the prestigious 'Bournemouth Belle' express.

*Right* **BOURNEMOUTH:** 'Merchant Navy' Class No 35008 *Orient Line* is seen at Bournemouth Central, having worked in from Weymouth.

*Above right* **GUILDFORD:** 'Charlies' were the nicknames given to the distinctive 'Q1' workhorses by Southern Railway crews – and there are certainly plenty of 'right Charlies' in this photograph, taken from the signal gantry at Guildford loco depot. In view are 'Q1' Nos 33035, 33022, 33039, 33032 and 33001, as well as a 1921 Urie 'S15' 4-6-0 and a Standard Class 4 4-6-0. Such a sight will never be seen again.

**HAVANT:** The ubiquitous 'Terrier' 0-6-0T tank engines were an everyday sight on Southern rails, undertaking all sorts of duties. Here's turnover engine No 32678 at Havant on 19 August (*right*), and about to leave with the 12.05pm service to Hayling Island (*below*).

*Left* **BATH:** Passengers on the 'Pines Express' were greeted with this sight as they coasted into Bath Green Park station on 24 August – the busy loco yard containing Standard Class 5 4-6-0 No 73054, a 'Standard 4' 2-6-0, an S&D 2-8-0 and a 'Standard 3' 2-6-2T all on display.

*Below* **BLANDFORD FORUM:** We're well on Somerset & Dorset metals now as the 'Pines Express' leaves Blandford Forum, headed by Standard Class 5 4-6-0 No 73052.

*Opposite* **GUILDFORD:** Early September saw some unusual locomotives around the area as special excursions from all over the country descended upon Surrey for the Farnham Air Show. It's 7 September and ex-LMS 4-6-0 No 44847 from Leicester has arrived in Guildford yard after working a special from Doncaster.

**COWES:** We're on the Isle of Wight now, enjoying a great view of engine No 20, named *Shanklin*, about to depart with the 5.24pm service to Ryde.

# 1962 Happenings (4)

### November
- The United Nations passes a resolution condemning South Africa's apartheid policies and calls on UN member states to cease military and economic relations with the nation
- In response to the Soviet Union agreeing to remove its missiles from Cuba, US President John F. Kennedy ends the blockade of the Caribbean nation
- Satire show *That Was The Week That Was* is broadcast on the BBC
- An agreement is signed between Britain and France to develop the Concorde supersonic aircraft

### December
- David Lean's epic film *Lawrence of Arabia*, starring Peter O'Toole and Omar Sharif, premieres in London
- Britain agrees to purchase Polaris missiles from the US
- The biggest freeze in living memory hits Britain. There are no frost-free nights from 22 December until 5 March 1963

*Left* **DUNFERMLINE** We're in Scotland now, and here's very grimy-looking 'A1' 'Pacific' No 60162 *Saint Johnstoun* leaving Dunfermline and heading north for Perth and Inverness. Some 49 'A1s' were built to the design of the LNER's CME Arthur Peppercorn during the early British Railways era, but all were scrapped and none survived into preservation. However, enthusiasts decided to built a brand-new 'A1' locomotive from scratch and, in 2008, No 60163 *Tornado* was completed and now runs on Britain's main lines.

*Below* **TAY BRIDGE:** Here's a shot of the Tay Bridge taken from a railcar heading for Dundee – scene of one of Britain's most notorious railway disasters. It occurred on the night of 28 December 1879, when the first bridge collapsed during a storm while a train was passing over it; all 75 people on the train were killed. In the aftermath, a sturdier bridge, able to withstand the high winds that roar down the Firth of Tay, was built to replace the original.

*Right* **DUNDEE** Class 'J36' 0-6-0 No 65319 stands in Dundee loco yard on 17 September.

# OCTOBER A Pullman

## feast to divert us...

*Left* **SANDHURST HALT:** Back in Surrey on 30 September, here's 'N' Class 2-6-0 No 31862 leaving Sandhurst Halt with the 4.54pm train bound for Reading

*Below left* **EXMOUTH:** This snapshot, taken from the passing 4.55pm express from Exeter Central to Waterloo on Sunday 14 October, gives a wonderful view of the elements that made up a typical motive power depot in the early 1960s. A giant coaler dominates the scene at Exmouth Junction (72A), which as recently as 1959 had housed 115 locomotives, including an impressive roster of 'West Country', 'Battle of Britain' and 'Merchant Navy' 'Pacifics'. But it was already in steep decline by the time this photograph was taken in 1962, when it became part of the Western Region (although the shed code was not changed to 85B until September 1963). The main engine shed, to the left of the coaler, was about to be demolished (today a supermarket stands on the site). The depot finally closed in May 1965, and the 23 locomotives that remained were moved to Templecombe, Gloucester, Worcester and Bristol Barrow Road.

*Right* **SANDHURST:** The reason for the decline of steam sheds was, of course, the demise of steam locomotives. They were already being replaced with electric and, in this case, diesel traction. Here is D6568 hauling a northbound express through Little Sandhurst on 25 October.

*Below* **PORTSMOUTH:** Photographer Ray gave his mother a surprise on 28 October – he treated her to lunch on the 'Bournemouth Belle'. Here she is enjoying the Pullman service, complete with attentive conductor. In case you're wondering what the Waterloo-Bournemouth service was doing on the Portsmouth line, it had been diverted due to Sunday engineering works.

*Left* **BURITON:** Here's the same train, descending from Buriton. Ray leaned out of the window to snap this photograph of the ten glorious Pullman cars rounding the curve. The train is being hauled by 'West Country' 'light Pacific' No 34010 *Sidmouth*, which had been built in Brighton in September 1945. You can't see it very well in this photograph, but you will be able to in the future, for it has led a chequered career since it was withdrawn in March 1945. After rusting in Barry scrapyard in South Wales for several decades, it was purchased in 1982 and moved to the North Yorkshire Moors Railway, where it was earmarked for restoration. However, after 15 years in limbo the remains of the locomotive were acquired by Southern Locomotives Ltd of Swanage, who are hoping to begin restoration in 2013.

*Above* **GUILDFORD:** 'West Country' Class 'light Pacific' No 34095 *Brentor* pulls away from Guildford on a diverted Sitmar Line boat express from Southampton to London. This locomotive was built by the newly nationalised British Railways in October 1949 and rebuilt in January 1961. It was among the last to be scrapped, in July 1967.

# NOVEMBER Through Mid Wales for Shrewsbury, Sugar loaf, Swansea...

*Above* **EFFINGHAM:** 'Battle of Britain' Class No 34089 *602 Squadron* arrives at Effingham Junction on a Ramblers' Special to Shalford, Chilworth and Comshall on 4 November. Built at Eastleigh Works in 1948, this engine was scrapped in 1967.

*Right* **LLANDRINDOD WELLS:** Ray took a trip to Wales in November. This is BR 5MT 4-6-0 No 73026, heading the 11.45am Shrewsbury to Swansea train at Llandrindod Wells on the 16th. Some 172 of these engines were built at BR's Derby and Doncaster works between April 1951 and June 1957. They were withdrawn from service between 1964 and June 1968, with all but five scrapped. Unfortunately, No 73026 was not among the survivors.

*Left* **LLANDEILO:** The lovely town of Llandeilo overlooks the Tywi valley in central Wales. Nearby, the scenic Central Wales line (today the Heart of Wales line) ascends the famous Sugar Loaf Bank, a long, 1-in-60 climb that pushed heavily laden steam engines to the limit. Here are Nos 45422 (ex-Swansea) and 73026 (ex-Shrewsbury) at the summit of the bank.

*Above* **LLANDEILO:** The previous photograph was taken from Sugar Loaf Summit signal box, seen here.

*Above right* **SWANSEA VICTORIA:** No 73026, seen opposite at Sugar Loaf Summit, arrives at Swansea Victoria from Shrewsbury.

*Left* **GUILDFORD:** Back on the Southern Region on 17 November, here's 'U' Class 2-6-0 No 31635, which has recently been rebuilt with outside steam pipes and a complete new front end, including cylinders and frames. This venerable engine was one of 50 built between 1928 and 1931, to the design of Richard Maunsell.

# DECEMBER The train now freezing at platform...

**Below DONCASTER:** Our photographer's quest for steam took him all over the country – and at no time more so than the first half of December. Here, on the first day of the month, he captured ex-LNER 'A4' No 60017 *Silver Fox* about to leave Doncaster on the northbound 'White Rose' express. This class of 'Pacifics' is probably the most famous ever built, for it included *Mallard*, the locomotive that on 3 July 1938 set the world speed record for steam of 126mph. A total of 35 'A4s' were built, to the design of Sir Nigel Gresley. *Silver Fox* was the fourth to be built – the first four all having 'silver' in their names, as they were intended to haul the prestigious 'Silver Jubilee' train. Soon after this photograph was taken, *Silver Fox* was withdrawn; alas, it was not among the six 'A4s' that were preserved.

**Right WATERLOO:** The following day, back at London's Waterloo station, Ray photographed Beattie well tank No 30585 about to depart with an SLS and RCTS rail tour to Hampton Court, Shepperton and Chessington. The smartly dressed dignitaries are motive power superintendent Grimes (left) and motive power inspector Bollom. The venerable 2-4-0 engine they are inspecting dated back to 1874, when it was among 85 built for the former London & South Western Railway for passenger services in the capital's suburbs. It was designed by the LSWR's Mechanical Engineer, Joseph Beattie.

**Right RIBBLEHEAD:** It's 10 December, and today we're on the southbound 'Thames-Clyde Express', crossing the famous Ribblehead Viaduct on the Settle-Carlisle line in North Yorkshire. Designed by the engineer John Crossley to cross the valley of the upper River Ribble, work began on the viaduct in 1870. It is 104 feet high and a quarter of a mile long, comprises 24 arches and was completed in 1874. A

century of exposure to the harsh weather of the upland moors saw the viaduct fall into poor repair – so much so that British Rail attempted to close it in the 1980s. However, the outcry was so great that the viaduct was repaired and the line – regarded as the most scenic in England – was reprieved.

*Above* **KILMARNOCK:** Later the same day Ray arrived in Kilmarnock, where he captured this atmospheric images of an ex-LMS Class 5 4-6-0 shunting coaching stock.

*Right* **CHESSINGTON:** On 16 December he was back in Surrey – at Chessington South, to be exact – where he snapped the very last Urie 'H16' Class 4-6-2T about to depart on an RCTS tour. No 30517 was the second of just five of these versatile tank engines built by the LSWR at Eastleigh Works between November 1921 and February 1922, to the design of Robert Urie. None survived into preservation.

*Above right* **GUILDFORD:** Here's an even more unusual tank engine – 'USA' Class 0-6-0 No 30072 – pictured at Guildford. This locomotive had recently been retired from active service at Southampton Docks, where diesel motive power had replaced steam.

*Right* **BOURNEMOUTH WEST:** On 22 December the most severe freeze since the 18th century seized the entire country and this was the scene at Bournemouth West on the 28th, which had already suffered severe blizzards. 'Standard 4' 2-6-0 No 76013 is pictured with the front portion of the 2.20pm express to Waterloo. This engine worked only as far as Bournemouth Central, where the coaches were uncoupled and added to the train from Weymouth – usually a 'Merchant Navy' Class 4-6-2 – which continued to the capital.